curiou♀about

FERRETS

BY ALISSA THIELGES

AMICUS

What are you

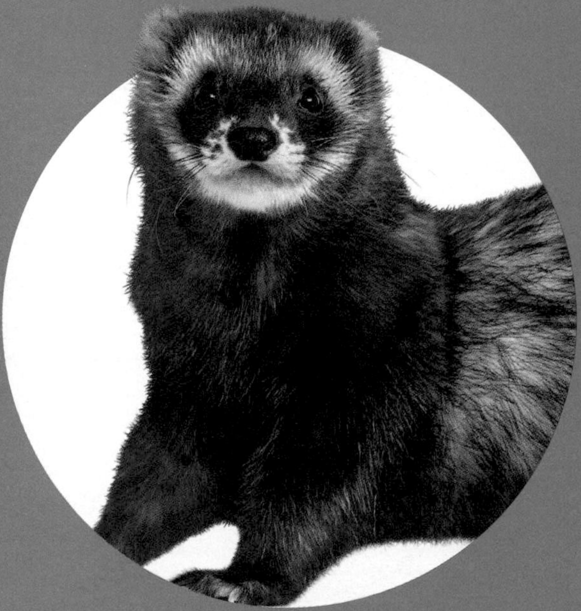

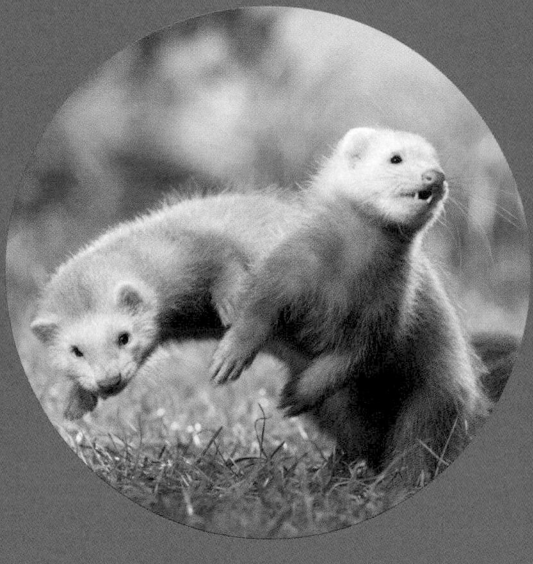

curious about?

CHAPTER THREE

Playing with a Ferret

PAGE
16

Curious About is published by Amicus
P.O. Box 227
Mankato, MN 56002
www.amicuspublishing.us

Editor: Rebecca Glaser
Series Designer: Kathleen Petelinsek
Book Designer: Aubrey Harper
Photo Researchers: Alissa Thielges and Omay Ayres

Library of Congress Cataloging-in-Publication Data
Names: Thielges, Alissa, 1995– author.
Title: Curious about ferrets / by Alissa Thielges.
Description: Mankato, Minnesota : Amicus,
[2023] | Series: Curious about
pets | Includes bibliographical references
and index. | Audience: Ages 6–9
| Audience: Grades 2–3 | Summary: "Nine
kid-friendly questions and answers
teach readers about life with a pet ferret,
including their behavior, playful antics,
and tendency to run into walls. Simple
infographics support visual learning. A
Stay Curious! feature encourages kids to keep
asking questions and models media
literacy skills. Includes table of contents, glossary,
and index."—Provided by publisher.
Identifiers: LCCN 2021059047 (print) |
LCCN 2021059048 (ebook) | ISBN
9781645493099 (hardcover) | ISBN
9781681528335 (paperback) | ISBN
9781645493976 (ebook)
Subjects: LCSH: Ferrets as pets–Juvenile literature.
Classification: LCC SF459.F47 T45 2023
(print) | LCC SF459.F47 (ebook) |
DDC 636.976/628–dc23/20211208
LC record available at https://lccn.loc.gov/2021059047
LC ebook record available at https://lccn.loc.gov/2021059048

Photo credits: Alamy/Giel, O./juniors@wildlife/2, 11 (top),
11 (bottom right), 13, 16, 18–19; iStock/cynoclub, 3, 15,
Delecrouix, 6–7, fotojagodka, cover, 1, 9, 11 (bottom left,
middle), GlobalP, 2, 4–5, 9, 12; Shutterstock/Liliana_Cantu,
8, IrinaK, 11, Ermolaev Alexander, 17, Karolsejnova, 21

Why do ferrets smell weird?

Ferrets have a good sense of smell.

Ferrets have oil **glands** on their skin. They give off a **musky** smell. This smell marks their home. Your pet rubs against its toys and cage. He is saying, "This is my home." Change your pet's bedding at least once a week. This will help so the smell isn't so strong.

DID YOU KNOW?
Ferrets can be trained to pee in a litter box like a cat.

Where do you keep a ferret?

Ferrets like company. You can keep two ferrets in the same cage.

A cage is a safe place. It should have different levels. A ferret eats and sleeps there. They sleep about 18 hours a day. Ferrets also need to be let out every day. They have a lot of energy. They need room to run and play.

How many kinds of ferrets are there?

A panda ferret has a white head and black shoulders, like a panda bear.

There is only one **species** of pet ferret. It comes in many different colors. It lives about seven years. There are also wild ferrets. The black-footed ferret lives in the United States. It is **endangered**.

SABLE

ALBINO

BLACK SABLE

CHAMPAGNE

BLACK

CHAPTER TWO

FERRET BEHAVIOR

What sounds does a ferret make?

Ferrets are pretty quiet. They make soft sounds. A happy ferret clucks softly. This sound is called dooking. They do this when dancing around. A scared or angry ferret will hiss. Its tail puffs out. It may also bark loudly.

Ferrets like to play outside.

Dook

DID YOU KNOW?
Ferrets dance for joy!
If your ferret jumps, runs,
hops, and rolls around,
it is very happy.

Hop sideways

Roll on the floor

Why do ferrets run into walls and furniture?

A ferret zooms around a room. He darts and dashes. He jumps on furniture. He zooms—right into a wall! Ferrets are clumsy. They only see a few feet in front of them. They can't tell how close something is. When they go too fast, they run into things.

A ferret will hide
while playing.

Why does my ferret hide her toys?

She is **hoarding**. Wild ferrets do this after a hunt. They drag their food to their den. The food stays safe. Your pet will stash her food and favorite toys. She hides them in her cage. She may even take your stuff!

A ferret will crawl through a tunnel and chase balls.

DID YOU KNOW?

Wild ferrets eat meat. Pets eat mainly ferret pellets.

What do ferrets like to do?

A ferret lov
to explore c
of its cag

Explore! Ferrets are very smart. They like puzzles and mazes. Wild ferrets live in tunnels. A long tube is a great toy. Your pet will love crawling through them. Just make sure she doesn't get stuck.

DID YOU KNOW?

Anything can be a ferret toy: stuffed animals, crinkly paper balls, even a string to chase.

My ferret bites when we play. Why?

He is excited. Ferrets play rough. They bite each other. Their skin is thick, so it doesn't hurt. A ferret may nip your toes. He wants to chase! If you don't like this, say, "No." Then play with a toy. He will bite that instead of you.

Ferrets fight when they play.

Can I take my ferret outside?

Yes. Outside play is great. There are new smells. Ferrets can go on walks just like a dog. Make sure your pet wears a harness with a leash. You don't want her to run away.

Ferrets prefer cool weather. Don't take them out when it's very hot.

ASK MORE QUESTIONS

What treats can I feed a ferret?

Where can I find black-footed ferrets?

Try a BIG QUESTION: How do wild animals become pets?

SEARCH FOR ANSWERS

Search the library catalog or the Internet.
A librarian, teacher, or parent can help you.

Using Keywords
Find the looking glass.

🔍

Keywords are the most important words in your question.

?

If you want to know about:

- what ferrets can eat, type: FERRET DIET

- where to find black-footed ferrets, type: BLACK-FOOTED FERRET RANGE

FIND GOOD SOURCES

Here are some good, safe sources you can use in your research.
Your librarian can help you find more.

Books
Can I Keep It? Small Pets Guide
by Tanguy, 2020.

My Pet Ferret
by Paige V. Polinsky, 2020.

Internet Sites
Questions about Black-Footed Ferrets
*https://nationalzoo.si.edu/animals/
news/what-do-black-footed-ferrets-sound-
and-other-ferret-questions-answered*
The Smithsonian National Zoo leads animal
research and conservation efforts.

**What Do Ferrets Eat? A Guide
to Feeding Your Ferret**
*https://www.petmd.com/ferret/
nutrition/evr_ft_nutrition_ferret*
PetMD has articles written by veterinarians
on pet care and advice.

Every effort has been made to ensure that these
websites are appropriate for children. However,
because of the nature of the Internet, it is impossible
to guarantee that these sites will remain active
indefinitely or that their contents will not be altered.

SHARE AND TAKE ACTION

Go to an exotic pet show.
There will be all sorts of unusual
pets. You can ask the owners
how they care for their pets.

**Offer to pet sit
for a neighbor.**

**Raise money for
black-footed ferrets.**
Be a role model for supporting
endangered species.

**Visit ferrets at a zoo
or pet store.**
Ask workers how they
care for ferrets.

GLOSSARY

endangered Describes an animal with a very low population that could die out.

gland An organ in the body that makes chemicals and releases a fluid or smell.

hoarding To collect and store things.

musky Having a strong-smelling odor.

species A group of living things with similar features that are grouped under a common name and can make babies.

INDEX

About the Author

Alissa Thielges is a writer and editor in southern Minnesota who hopes to inspire kids to stay curious about their interests. She doesn't own any pets but would love to have a turtle and dog someday.